tiny love stories

tiny love stories

True Tales of Love in 100 Words or Less

Edited by Daniel Jones and Miya Lee
of Modern Love in The New York Times

artisan | new york

Contents

About Modern Love

Modern Love is a weekly personal essay column about relationships, feelings, betrayals and revelations that began appearing in The New York Times in 2004. In 2016, the column became a weekly podcast; after debuting at #1 on iTunes, it has been downloaded nearly 100 million times. A book of collected columns—*Modern Love: True Stories of Love, Loss, and Redemption*—was published in 2019, the same year Amazon Studios released the first season of its *Modern Love* streaming series, an eight-episode show based on the column.

What Are Tiny Love Stories?

Tiny Love Stories began as a challenge from the editors of Modern Love at The New York Times: "What kind of love story can you share in two tweets, an Instagram caption or a Facebook post? Tell us a love story from your own life—happy or sad, capturing a moment or a lifetime—in no more than 100 words." Soon we editors were inundated with submissions, each no longer than the introduction you are now reading. This book contains many of the most delightful and moving stories we received. We hope you enjoy them. Consider submitting your own at nytimes.com/tinylovestories.

THE STORIES

My Main Men as Meals

My first boyfriend, Howie, was matzo ball soup: warm and homey, wonderful on a cold, wintry day, but not a lot of sex appeal. My previously married ex-husband, John, was leftover fast food: so compelling in the refrigerator, but you were always sorry after eating it. Vinnie, pizza-maker and "transition man," was a banquet verging on bacchanal: destined to create heartburn but impossible to stop eating. My now and hopefully forever man, Charles, is bran flakes sprinkled with a few Lucky Charms: He keeps me regular and, on most days, is magically delicious.

—Jill Lipton

Clockwise from top left: Chris, me, Greg and Kurt at our childhood home in Kansas City.

When We Became One

We grew up in even numbers. Two parents, four sons, six people. Two boys per bedroom. Summers with two of us at one of our grandparents' houses and two at the other, then a switch. Always disciplined, referred to and taught about the facts of life in pairs. Then, in middle age, Kurt called me to say that Greg, the youngest, had unexpectedly died, and I called Chris to tell him. Chris and I flew home, and Kurt met us at the airport. We held each other, and in that moment, four became three became one. —Brian Justice

All-Nighters, Cake, and Netflix

For a decade, I've watched my former classmates settle into the conventional domestic pattern: husband, wife, baby, house. They look grown up now. They look like their parents. I, however, remain single at 34, pulling all-nighters and eating cake for dinner. I drive an hour for good ramen. I skip town for the weekend. I watch Netflix with impunity. No one is angry about dirty dishes. Marriage sent my classmates down a steadier path, one that rarely crosses my itinerant course. I do miss them. For me, saying "Congratulations on your engagement" is too often another way of saying "Goodbye."

—Adam Chandler

The Folly of Date Night

Date night! Tonight we are free! No bottoms to wipe or mouths to feed; it's just you and me. "We should go out," I say. "Run naked in the rain, make love on a train or something." But we don't. Instead, we look at pictures of the children on our phones until we fall asleep.
                                                    —Emily-Jane Clark

He Tried So Hard to Remember Me

When my 61-year-old father learned he had Alzheimer's, we went to CVS together and bought the largest stack of notecards they sold. I asked, "What's the town where you grew up?" We wrote Union Springs, Alabama. I asked, "Who was your first kiss?" Amanda. Four years later, preparing to move my father into memory care, I packed up his desk. Taking the notecards felt silly, so I wrapped the long-forgotten stack in a rubber band and opened his drawer to toss them away. Inside, I found more notecards. They all said the same thing: my name.   —Drew Hasson

Don't Send Nudes

We were online content moderators taking down nude photos. All day, we sorted through thousands of photos and messages flagged as inappropriate on a meet-up app. He sat nearby, but our office had a strict no-talking rule, so our relationship began in silence as we sent each other funny things we found via Gchat. This led to more messaging until one day we grew tired of talking about nudes and decided to see each other naked instead.

—Kristine Murawski

Our relationship was reassembled with tape.

Torn Up

"I'm leaving you," she said. Regrettably dramatic, I yanked the photo from its frame and tore it into pieces. Taken the night we first met, the photo was irreplaceable. I imagined tears, then a change of course, reconciliation. Instead, she discarded the shredded pieces in a wastebasket. It's true what they say: The heart can break. Eventually, I reclaimed the pieces and, with tape, carefully reassembled the image. She did leave. Months passed. She came back. My heart mended. The patchwork is in a frame above our couch and reminds us of the fragility of love.

—Susan Anderson

Who Cares Less?

He hooked up with someone else. I never texted first. He didn't show up to meet my sister. I was still talking to my ex. We were stuck in a game of Who Cares Less? I won. But really, I lost.   —Caroline Kulig

Our Love Tripod

On the eve of the new millennium, I fell in love with Andrew, a dashing English ad executive. Inconveniently, I didn't fall out of love with Scott, an American architectural photographer and my longtime partner. Our dilemma resulted in an unexpected and enduring romance: a V-shaped love triangle sans vows and offspring. Born English, now a naturalized American, I am the hinge in our harmonious household of three: I sleep with both men; they each sleep with only me. We share everything else—home, finances, friends, vacations, life-threatening calamities. As Scott says, our tripod is more stable than a bipod. —Kate Holt

I Didn't Run

I met David on a blind date. The next day, I invited him over for tea. He appeared on my porch, peeking through the glass, offering me his cupped palms. "It's all yours," he said. "What? Sweaty hands?" "No." He beamed. "My heart." Typically, this would make me run, but I didn't. He had picked me to hold his heart. His body was ravaged with cancer, but still, I accepted. We laughed. We cried. We married. Twenty-two months after our eyes met, I stood at the river, cupping my palms with ashes, and let go. —Susan Purvis

"Are You Sure He Was Boring?"

Five years of online dating. Countless dates. Zero butterflies. Zero boyfriends. Definitely zero husbands. So close to finding love, they say. You never know, they say. Don't judge him by his looks; you should give his personality a chance. Are you sure he was boring? Maybe he was just having an off day. Countless excuses. Zero accountability. Zero consistency. Definitely zero expectations. The current state of dating for 30-something women: Oh, you haven't found love yet? You aren't looking hard enough.   —Shruti Gupta

Happy together.

Inseparable Twins

Sick of being "the twins," we made rules for freshman year. Keep my hair short and red, Anushka's brown and long. Live in different dorms. Sit on opposite sides of lecture halls (we're both biology majors). No eating in the same dining hall or going to the same parties. Meet once a week, max. That didn't last. I couldn't live apart from someone who's a part of me. After a year of enduring impossible problem sets, roommate drama, assorted heartbreaks and our parents' divorce, we laugh at how we once thought we'd do it alone.

—Anjali Walia

One Obvious Pro

I grew up in a small town where same-sex relationships were considered abnormal and wrong. As I struggled with my sexuality, I began wondering, "Should I even try to have a romantic relationship?" When I left for college and fell for a girl, I was afraid to act on my feelings. My friend John came to my dorm to help me weigh the pros and cons of pursuing her. Later, I looked over the list by myself. John had written mostly jokes, except for one word: "Love?"

—Gabriella Vacarelo

Planting Perennials

After I asked my husband to leave, after nights of holding my weeping daughters, after clumps of hair came out in my hands, my mother came to visit. She shook her head. "I don't understand. In sickness and in health!" The next morning, I found her in my scraggly yard. Digging, weeding, sowing. When her stay was over, the tidiness rattled me: fresh mulch, trimmed trees, perfectly rounded shrubs. I thought that by planting perennials, she was saying, "These will return, in spite of you." But maybe, instead: "Here; this will be easier."

—Lisa Mecham

Separate Vacations

He took a boat. I stayed home. Married forty-one years, we don't mind going our separate ways. Later he told me stories about the Canadian lake, a cedar boat, the fish he gently let go. I wrote a tiny story about his love of nature. It began: He took a boat. It ended: We are happy when alone together.

—Beverly Blasingame

A Scarier Kind of Gravity

How to meet cute: (1) Exploit Tinder to deal with your fidgety fingers. (2) Make plans to meet in Central Park, but don't send your location ("Let's play hide-and-seek: black dress"). (3) Withhold your outrage when he gives up and says to look for him instead. (4) Spin in frustrated circles until you spot him on top of a rock. (5) Instantly overcome your fear of heights to climb to him. (6) Over the next three hours, succumb to a much different, much scarier kind of gravity. (7) Delete Tinder.

—Linh Nguyen

Not Done with the World

After five rounds of in vitro fertilization, my wife and I didn't have the funds to be parents anymore. We cried all the time. Avoided Facebook. Held our dogs too tight. Watched baby elephant videos. To escape the wormhole of grief, we bought tickets to Prague we could barely afford. Our sadness flickered like a ghost. In the Old Town, we smiled. Licked the rain from each other's lips. Kissed on Charles Bridge. Wrote graffiti declaring our love. Held hands on the tram. Ate soup that warmed our bones. We were not done with the world.

—Jackson Bliss

"Get Up. It's OK."

In kindergarten, I was asked what I wanted to be when I grew up. "A mother," I wrote, drawing a prim lace dress and an apron. "That's not a profession," my teacher said. Twenty years later, motherhood for me descended into madness. Psychiatric illness is a cruel thing, a paralysis. While I was in bed, my young son approached. "Get up," he said. This would become my mantra, from therapy to rehabilitation. Now, on cool fall mornings, we say it to each other as we practice hockey together. "Get up. It's OK. I'm right here with you."

—Mollie Garnes

Selfie taken on the corner of Twenty-Second Street and Eighth Avenue in New York City.

That Big Gorgeous Life

After the breakup, we spent every Thanksgiving, birthday and Christmas together. Close enough to touch, legs inches apart. We were still dying of AIDS in the '90s, but I always thought no, not Michael. When he died, I wondered who would love black gay me like that ever again. It's taken me twenty years to see what he saw in me. That big gorgeous life was too beautiful to be in ruins. Damn it, Michael. And yet I can still hear you saying, "Get off the cross, Mary. Somebody else needs the wood." Just as close as two legs almost touching.

—Wesley Rowell

Passing the Message On

As I waited for my friend to pay the bill, an elderly gentleman said, "Excuse me. I want you to know that you make a lovely couple. My wife recently passed. Someone said this to us when we were dating. I'm passing it on to you." We weren't dating. But just thirty minutes earlier, my friend had suggested we consider doing so. I was unsure, fearful of losing the friendship. I am forever grateful to that beautiful man who touched my heart that day. My friend, who became my husband, recently died. I am looking to pass the message on. —Kathy Caruso

Luckily, There Was No Facilitator

It was 2000. I was a sad middle-aged social worker nervously attending a divorce support group at an Episcopal church in Atlanta. Only one other person was there, a man my age, talkative. We purged our agony for hours and I thought, "Geez, this facilitator is so self-disclosing." Then he said, "How long have you been running this group?" The real leader never came that day we shared our heartache and felt the first frisson of love. We laughed all the way to the parking lot and never went back to the group.   —Moira Keller

Way Before *La La Land*

It was much too early to be awake, but I had a long commute from Tujunga to Marina del Rey. The 405 was stopped (this was way before *La La Land*). Suddenly, the driver door of the car directly in front of my Toyota swung open. The man I had gone out with for the first time the night before emerged and walked toward me. He kissed me through my window, then strolled back to his car. Traffic began to move. Now we are both old and have been married forever. But the memory holds. —Peg Burr

When Love Is a Recipe

Chopped celery and squared potatoes waiting in the fridge. On the counter, a jug of water and a slow cooker filled with dried peas. On the lid, a tiny note from my husband, the professional chef, to me, who burns water. "At noonish: (1) Add water. (2) Add veggies. (3) Stir. (4) Plug in. (5) Forget." His sweetly crooked handwriting. His unconditional faith in me. Between steps 4 and 5, it hit me. Married love is seldom about the grand gesture. Sometimes it simply shows up as a recipe from your partner, helping you make a tasty pot of soup.   —Meagan Fratiello

Dakota's Best Prom Date

I was Dakota's prom date so long as he could not "find anyone better." We are married now. I guess he couldn't.

—Megan Kline

Married Marines

We locked eyes across a crowded room. He was handsome in his military uniform; I was self-conscious in mine. A colleague at first, he earned my respect, my friendship and, finally, my heart. Years later, he faded away and she appeared. We picked out a new name for her. We shared wardrobes, sorrows, joys and passion as I fell in love with her graceful curves. I was mesmerized by the way she moved, black curls tumbling over her shoulders. My husband gone, now my wife holds my whole heart in her hands.

—Jacqueline Keavney Lader

No Such Thing as Effortless

My best friend and I started dating in high school. For six years, we cycled through breakups and reconciliations, brought back together by a mutual need for security. Our identities were so wrapped up in our relationship that we couldn't bear to imagine ourselves alone. She wanted therapy. I demurred, hung up on the seeming effortlessness of "good" relationships. So she broke things off, for good. Today, I'm a couple's therapist. The only thing more potent than this irony is my hope that our story isn't over yet.   —Jacob Wollinger

Off the Curb

I had been kicked to the curb at 52. Took that as an omen. No more love for me, and no point even looking. Then I sat down at a New Year's Eve party in the only empty chair in the room, a guy sitting beside me. Struck up a conversation, which was only polite, about our children—heads close together, given the noise. We have been talking now for ten years, heads close together. Lesson learned: Be open.

—Susan Lightstone

My mother and my daughter.

The Holiest of Communions

She no longer wore her thick glasses, her eyes watery and unsure. She could no longer feed herself. When we visited, my son, Mathias, fed her pureed vegetables a spoonful at a time. My tiny daughter, Christina, watched, then squeezed in between her brother and her grandma. First, Christina planted a kiss, the noisy, juicy kind Grandma used to give her. They giggled. Then Christina tore off a piece of soft bread and placed it on her grandma's tongue. Ma accepted it and swallowed. The sadness lifted. For me, it was the holiest of communions.

—Joyce Simon

Waiting for the Buffering to End

My boyfriend and I try to have a date night every weekend. Typical, except our dates span two time zones and 1,800 miles. I attend college in Ohio, and he in Arizona. Love, for us, has become FaceTiming during meals (so we don't have to eat alone), packing his favorite baked goods ever-so-tightly so they don't go stale in the mail, and pausing the Netflix movie because the other person's laptop is buffering. We sprint through the airport one way and trudge the other. It's not an easy relationship, but it's ours.   —Gina Deaton

Things Tinder Dates Offered Me

Jars of jam, help hanging shelves, a ride to the airport, a hangover sundae with peanuts, shortcuts across Durham, trips to Costco, a planning commissioner's phone number, a medical consultation, a visit to a Georgia O'Keeffe exhibit, sympathy, homemade pumpkin bread, stories about their mothers, long hugs that stay hugs. I thought online dating would be about physical need, but instead I've experienced so many small intimacies. Still about need. Almost about love.   —Sarah Morris

Come Back, Cat!

One morning, the cat didn't come back. We searched for Lionel most of a summer. We thought his tabby coloring was unique, but we later found his look-alikes around the corner, at shelters, online. Each time, our hearts soared. Lionel! He had been a needed gift for our youngest child. We never imagined he would disappear. Can you ever? Recently, an insistent tabby has been appearing on our doorstep, yowling. I texted his photo to the children, now grown. Could it be? No; too big, too gray, too long ago. His collar reads "River." He brings memories rushing back.

—Christine Kouwenhoven

An Unexpected Sign

I was 30 and knew I couldn't have a baby. Accompanying my pregnant friend shopping one day, I admired a striped onesie with a crab sewn on the backside. I told her if I ever had a son, I would want him to wear it. Eight days later, I went to church and saw an infant snuggled in his grandmother's arms. He was wearing the same onesie. At the end of the service, the reverend announced that the baby was in need of an immediate home. Two days later, he moved into mine. Now he's 5 and my son.

—Sarah Reynolds Westin

Timothy Is Waiting for Me

When I visit my parents in Arizona, I sleep in my childhood bedroom. The dogs are always happy to see me. On one trip, I decided to take an evening flight back to New York. I packed my belongings and said my goodbyes. Waiting in the airport security line, I opened a text my mother had sent: a picture of our Chihuahua waiting on the bed. I cried. It seemed that Timothy, who had slept next to me throughout my visit, had not been told that I had left.

—Elizabeth Hernandez

"Why Is He with Her?"

"She's pretty, for a dark-skinned girl." I heard this often growing up in skin-color-obsessed India. Nishanth and I met in college. He is a handsome, light-skinned man. He loved me for who I was and never considered my skin color. But friends, family and strangers did and wondered, some quietly, others aloud: "Why is he with her?" His family objected. What would people think if he were to bring a dark-skinned girl into their light-skinned family? We fought to be together. Twenty years and a son later, Nishanth still sees me, not my complexion.

—Deepthi Nishanth

Letting Him Go

At my father's funeral, people hugged my mother, sisters and me. With sad smiles, they shook their heads. A destructive arrhythmia had left my father brain-dead, just after he had rallied from a heart attack and bypass surgery. What a shame, they said. Yet beneath their condolences, I sensed unspoken questions: How could you do it? How could you disconnect his life support? Had they asked, we would have answered: Our love for him was mightier than our fear of losing him, mighty enough to gift him his freedom.

—Mary Liles Eicher

Oktoberfest Meet-Cute

We met in Munich during Oktoberfest. I had seen him the day I arrived, a handsome stranger exiting the train station. That night, we matched on a dating app but didn't connect. The next day, in a mass of beer drinkers dressed in traditional German clothes, I spotted him above the crowd, giving a toast atop a bench. We were wearing identical lederhosen. Slightly drunk, I pointed at him and said, "Hey you! Get down here!" As he jumped down, he said, "You found me!" I didn't even know I was looking for him, but two years later, I still have him.

—Ryan Leach

Our 5-year-old son, Luke.

Electric Blue Eyes

He was a senior with electric blue eyes. I was a sophomore with a crush. Introductions turned into lunch, then into a college romance. We were untouchable. But nights squeezed into my dorm bed turned into breakups and "I can't live without you" reunions. My senior year, two pink lines. He pawned his Martin guitar for a ring and sold his Jeep for a security deposit on a tiny Baltimore row house. I walked across the graduation stage 6 months pregnant. None of it has been perfect. But you know what is? The way our little boy looks at us with the same blue eyes.　　　—Elizabeth Mackey

Coming Out to My Son

I said to my 12-year-old son, "You know how men and women date and marry, like I did with Dad before we split up?" He nodded. "Well," I said, "I'm dating someone, but not a man; I'm dating a woman." He said, "Are you happy?" "Yes," I said. "Very happy." "Cool," he said. "Then I'm happy." A few years later, he walked me down the aisle to my soon-to-be wife.

—Carrie Platner

"The Storm Is Taking It All"

The winds of Hurricane Maria were barreling down our street in the mountain town of Cayey, Puerto Rico. The windows in my parents' bedroom began to shake. My mother left the room quickly, but my father froze. "I can't move," he said. "The storm is taking it all." My two siblings and I entered. We told him he needed to get out. "I can't," he said with a blank stare. We hugged him hard while the windows rattled, threatening to break loose. "Te tenemos, papi," we said. ("We got you, Dad.") He looked up at us and started walking.

—Melissa Alvarado Sierra

Trying Not to Love You

So far away from each other. An ocean and twenty years between us. "I love you, but we need to end whatever this is," she says. She may be right: We discuss the power imbalance between an older man and a younger woman, the age gap between her and my grown children. Months later, we are in the same city again for a day. It doesn't take a day. Not even a minute. Just a smile, and we are back where we started. In love, happy and confused. Confused because we're trying to fall in love with other people. And it isn't working.   —Nick Williamson

Climbing Mount Fuji

Huddled several kilometers up Mount Fuji, on a journey harder than we anticipated, Jeff looked into my eyes, which were blurry from crying, and said, "I wonder how many American Express points it would take to have a helicopter pick us up." Both of us exploded in laughter and tears. I dusted dirt off my body as he extended his hand and pulled me up. We continue up and down our mountain daily, in darkness and light, taking turns being the one holding out a hand and the one who needs lifting up to keep moving forward.   —Carrie Ferguson

A Second Chance at Young Love

I imagine my mother's engagement ring flashing in the lights of the Delta Upsilon parties she attended her senior year of college. Married right after graduation, my parents built a life together. While their 20-something friends spent nights gyrating to music in Manhattan clubs, my parents tried to find the perfect motion to rock me to sleep. A few decades later, I'm freshly graduated from college (sans engagement ring), and they're finally beginning to "date" again. At night, I lock the door behind them when they leave. —Delaney Tarpey

A Lifetime of Bliss

After a wedding in which our son was the best man, my wife and I were on the subway at midnight. A young man got on, continuing a conversation with a couple on the platform. He shouted, "Propose to her! Now! If you don't, someone else will." After the doors closed, he said to me, loudly, "He should propose, right?" After I agreed, he said, "See, even the old guy agrees with me!" Later, he added, "I hope I didn't embarrass you. But I want them to have what you have: a lifetime of bliss." How did he know?

—Dan Brody

My son playing at the Crissy Field Beach in San Francisco.

Out of the Dark, into the Sea

When the love of my life died of a heroin overdose, I believed love had left my life for good. Then I met Daniel. The relationship was everything I didn't think was going to work until late one night when he showed me where to find coyotes hiding in the San Francisco hills. His visa was expiring, so we got married at City Hall and celebrated with a giant cake from our local bakery. This love is not high drama, but the love for our baby boy is. Perhaps my boyfriend's death was the tragedy that allowed me to know the sound of my son's voice touching the sea.

—Molly Welton

Grandpa, I'm on the Toilet

My grandfather has dementia. When I was visiting, he barged into the bathroom to give me a newspaper clipping: an article about a boy who programmed robotic hands to play the piano. I guess he didn't remember that it is not OK to walk in on someone on the toilet, but he did remember that the piano is my favorite instrument. There are a lot of things we forget, I'm sure, but I don't think we ever really forget how to love each other.

—Bella O'Connor

Seeing Him in the
Chili Pepper Lights

It's that time again. How do I know? Because of that old string of red chili pepper lights from Albuquerque. We bought them more than thirty years ago for our first Christmas together, yet every one of those chilies still lights up when I plug them in. He's been gone six years now. Our love died before he did—at least officially, according to the divorce decree. But every Christmas, just like the red chili peppers, my heart glows red and I remember him.
                                              —Marla West

Our Gratitude Jar

We're supposed to open the jar on New Year's Day, hungover in our pajamas, reading the little notes of gratitude we write to each other throughout the year. But I haven't been able to wait. Every time I see him pause during a happy evening to write down a memory in his delicate script, I unscrew the jar, pull out the Post-it (despite his halfhearted protest) and smile as I read his words: gratitude for our health, our home, our family, our dog, our friendship and love. Why wait to remind ourselves how good life is together?

—Colleen Goodhue

Now It's All Fresh Fish

We are grandparents. The age when most couples stay put. "We need something new," I said as our frozen fish defrosted in our suburban Maryland kitchen. "Why not sell the house? We're retired, and the kids are settled. And you know it's been my dream to live abroad while we still can." My dream, not his. He looked at me, his face inscrutable. Three years, two funerals and two weddings later, we still eat fish for dinner. But now it's caught in Clew Bay, near our home in the shadow of Croagh Patrick. We're old, we're new, we're together, in Ireland.

—Roberta Beary

Storming into Kindergarten

It was the first of many first days of school. I walked in little steps toward the classroom, my parents striding beside me. Eager to take kindergarten by storm, I reminded myself that I had to make friends. I sat down next to a girl who was as tiny as I was. With my favorite topic in mind, I said, "Do you know my granny Alba?" My potential new friend's eyes opened wide with curiosity. My parents laughed by the door. I guess when you love someone so immensely, you assume that the rest of the world does too.

—Maria Paula Serrano

I Love a Man
with an Anchor Tattoo

Before leaving my studio apartment in Queens, I emailed my friends: "When I come back from Maine, I'll bring home a lobsterman with an anchor tattoo." I was joking, but once there, I spotted him—head to toe in yellow oilskins (just like a guy on a frozen fish box), climbing off his vintage Honda motorcycle. Now when he gets home from a day of fishing, our son runs into his arms, the right one tattooed with an anchor.   —Laura Serino

My son, Phil, and my father, Phillip, asleep on the D train.

Phil and Phillip

My son, Phil, and I came back to New York City
from Seattle for the holidays. We rode from
Manhattan to Brooklyn in a crowded subway
car. A stranger was kind enough to let my child
sit. Phil asked his grandpa Phillip to sit, and then
fell asleep on him. No other seats became available
during our hour-long ride. My father has
Parkinson's disease. He struggled but held my
son tightly. As we exited the train, his arms shook
with fatigue. Decades ago, that same man used
to rock me to sleep on packed trains. Those rides
were magical to a child.   —Kat Lieu

Boy Meets Girl. Girl and Girl Remain Madly in Love.

Boy meets girl. They date in college. Boy drops bombshell by taking job offer in Japan. Does she want to join? Girl thinks it over and decides to take a chance. They move to Japan, then the Philippines, then back to the United States. Boy becomes girl. Girl and girl remain madly in love years later.

—Ash Kline

Strangers on a Train

We met on a train from Paris to Barcelona. Sitting next to each other, we argued over who could use the power outlet. "Désolé, je crois que c'est à moi." ("Sorry, I think it's mine.") Instant crush. A perfect, flirtatious six hours. The beginning of our love story? We agreed to meet back in Paris: On March 19, I'd wait for his train at the Gare de Lyon railway station. We didn't know that coronavirus would confine us in different countries. Trusting in the power of the universe, we hadn't exchanged phone numbers. Sometimes, a romantic plan isn't enough. —Cecilia Pesao

No More Secrets

My grandmother never employed female pronouns when asking if I had found someone. She used the Spanish neutral pronouns to find out if that "someone" had arrived, if I was willing to introduce her to the person I loved. She never asked me if I was gay, but she didn't doubt it because she knew me better than anyone else. She took her silence to the grave, and now I face her gravestone with the boy she will never meet. Granny, today homosexuality is still taboo in Peru, but at least there are no more secrets between us.

—Marco Huarancca

"A Breakfast Betrayed"

We had been married just a few weeks. I used the last of the milk one morning and left for work while my husband was still in the shower. I returned that evening to find an art installation on the table, labeled in neat handwriting on a folded-over notecard: "A Breakfast Betrayed. 1993. Wheat on ceramic." Next to it was the bowl of cereal my husband had poured for himself—sitting milk-less. For more than twenty-five years, we have continued to treat domestic annoyances with humor. Our love has lasted; but even better, so has the fun.

—Mary Janevic

More Than Broken Kitchenware

Our first night living together, Steve accidentally broke my small colander. It was the first purchase I'd made for my college-bound self the summer after my mother's suicide. I had coped with her death with a controlled self-sufficiency. Watching that piece of plastic fly out of Steve's hands and crack on the floor, I felt my fragile facade of security breaking too. But amid my tears, Steve only wanted to understand why a $12 piece of kitchenware was connected to my pain. He isn't scared to peek into the darkest layers of my life. Steve sees me as my full self.

—Elizabeth Jones

A Small Hand in Mine

At first, she was the little face I saw in pictures when her mother and I began dating. When the time was right, she was the tiny body standing cautiously in the corner of the living room—wondering, waiting. Before long, she was the small hand in mine as we crossed the street, the smile to prove she had brushed her teeth and the curious voice whispering until we fell asleep. It began to feel as if she were mine. Now, six months after the split with her mother, I realize she was not mine. But I loved her.

—Nicole DeMouth

The photo that started everything.

The Most Important Photo Ever

Neither of us wanted to be at our high school reunion. I was worried that I would have to retell the story of my high school sweetheart's death from pancreatic cancer over and over. My former classmate was recently separated after years of being unhappily married. We didn't know each other in high school, but thirty years later, there we were, two lonely souls circling each other in a crowded room for hours until he took a photograph of me. We talked for two minutes, and it turned into a second lifetime. "The most important photo I've ever taken," he said. —Stacey Paterson-Korynkiewicz

They Took My Guts

On Valentine's Day, there was a sharp pain where there shouldn't be. It had taken guts to call off my engagement, and that's exactly what it cost me. "Your colon has to come out," the doctors said. I wanted to tell them to take my heart too. Two weeks after I discovered my fiancé's secret addiction, stress worsened my colitis to the point that I needed emergency surgery. My parents slept upright in plastic chairs next to my hospital bed. Mom's hand moved over mine, and Dad's body slumped toward the monitor. This is love, this is love, went my heart.

—Bethany Sales

A Warm Meal for My Brother

My big brother and I giggled at our successful dis-
obedience as we traded comic books, flashlights
bobbing between our beds. He was my friend, the
two of us bonded by years of childhood mischief.
Decades later, leaving a blues venue, I realized it had
been six years since I'd known my brother's where-
abouts. He would have loved the performance.
Outside, a stranger approached. "Spare five dollars
for a sandwich?" he asked. Looking into his eyes,
I wondered when my homeless brother had last
savored a warm meal. To this stranger's delight, I
pulled out a twenty. That night, I fed my brother.

— Cassandra Lund

My Husband Is Not My Son

Ever since I turned 45, my husband, who is nine months younger than I am, has been repeatedly mistaken for my son. I have two 20-something sons, but Mike is not one of them. I can't say that I've taken it well—or accepted it without a struggle. Botox has softened my lines, though my outlook has softened, too. Now, at 56, I see my husband's thick hair, slim physique and smooth skin as a bonus of being his partner. It makes me feel desirable. Thirty-two years ago, we chose each other. We choose each other still.

—Jane Marion

Wingwoman Captures Cockatoo

On holiday in America, I became pen pals with a guy who loves Aussie wildlife. Back in Sydney, I told my 85-year-old grandmother I wanted to send him photos of native birds. Weeks later, I received a voice mail message from her, saying, "I took my first photo! It's a cockatoo for you to send to that boy you like in New York." It was blurry, and his response wasn't game-changing, but I'll always remember that my grandmother learned how to use an iPhone just so she could help me impress a bloke overseas. The ultimate wingwoman.

—Hayley Noble

The Lavender Was Too Short

I had a bad summer cold. It was my idea to go to the lavender farm. The lavender was shorter than I imagined. I couldn't smell a damn thing. We were in the right place at the wrong time. Or maybe the wrong place altogether. We had taken a trip, thinking a long weekend would help. Though there were things that were right about our marriage, it was becoming increasingly wrong. The getaway was full of drama, tears, great food and a breathtaking sunset. It was our last vacation together. In that place, on that weekend, an ending became right.

—Michelle Pomerleau

Pierce My Ears or Run Away?

The kitchen whiteboard was erased, replaced by our 7-year-old's survey: "Isabel is going to get her ears perst or run away. Wich one do you choose?" "P. S. Once you choose you have to let her do it!!" Then a chart, with choices: "ears perst" or "runaway." "Put a ✔ in the spase you want." To her older brother: "Jeff, you have to do it as if you incredibly cared for me." Lastly: "P.S. I don't care if I spell thing rong." Proud of Isabel's defiance and ingenuity, my wife and I eventually let her get her ears "perst."

—Robert Schroeder

"Come Back,
Come Back, Come Back"

My brother going off to war in Afghanistan—
a modern Odysseus—unexpectedly transformed
me into Penelope. Just as Penelope wove a never-
ending shroud while she waited for her soldier
to come home, I developed a new and sudden
obsession with knitting, winding yarn around
needles to make my soldier an endless stream of
impractical and unwanted accessories—scarves,
gloves, even a camouflage hat (with pom-poms).
Powerless to protect him, I turned the rows of
stitches into my rosary: "Come back, come back,
come back." Once he was home, I put down my
needles, permanently.   —Kate Sturla

"Got Everything?" "Got You."

After forty-one years of marriage, those are not stars in our eyes, just light reflecting off our glasses. When you're young, you fight over children or money, but sex cures everything, and the future is far away. As you age, you fight over truly listening to each other, and the future has parked in your driveway. You take advantage, but you also learn to treasure each other while you're both still here. For years, upon leaving home, Bill has asked, "Got everything?" And I've said, "Got you—that's all I need." Somewhere along the way, it became true.

—Mary Ann Perri

The photo taken by a kind stranger.

Can I Take Your Picture?

When the days are so long and you finally get to the weekend and realize it's been months since you have been out with your partner without your little one too (beloved though she is), a stranger asks, "Hey, when is the last time you took a photo together?" You smile because you can't remember when the last time was, and you do find him pretty cute, even if you two fight sometimes and say things you shouldn't. The camera flashes, and you come back to each other and to the fact that love doesn't fail even when you do. —Fantasia Norse

Waiting for Frieda

After everyone had gone to bed, my 96-year-old aunt Frieda would slip on her red high-heeled slippers, peek out of her nursing-home-room door and run naked to her beloved Shottsy, a fellow resident. In her mind, he was my uncle Joe, her husband who had died thirty years before. Shottsy would expect my aunt's visits, lying under his covers in anticipation. One night, Shottsy shrieked when she arrived. Aunt Frieda had the frosting from her dinner-tray cake spread across her breasts. The nursing home called me with concern. Aunt Frieda insisted it was their anniversary.

—Maya Balle

What I Have Now

Things I used to have: A tidy résumé. Unfettered relationships. Nice hair. A paycheck. An almost complete disregard for anyone besides myself. An intact perineum. Steadfast opinions on child rearing. A self-regulating internal body temperature. A vague disdain for that mother who would "work from home" on Fridays even though our office did not have an established work-from-home-on-Fridays policy. An unwavering reverence for that old chestnut of the capitalist patriarchy, "I can have it all!" The slightest idea of who I am, or who I will become. Things I have now: A baby.   —Lesley Foster

City Boy Crashes Through Country Garage

I felt like such a city boy when we visited her family farm in Collie, New South Wales. Born and raised in Sydney's inner city, I had no dust on my boots or dirt under my nails. "You drive a ute?" her grandfather asked me, referring to a utility vehicle. "Absolutely," I lied. When I crashed through the back of their garage, I figured we were over. At least it would make a good story: "I used to date this girl until her grandfather killed me." He ran over, unleashing an impressive torrent of curse words. Then I saw her doubled over laughing and knew everything would be OK. —Thomas Mitchell

Food = Love

Every month, my family comes together at the same Korean barbecue restaurant in Bayside, Queens. My mother fills my plate with pieces of short rib faster than I can eat. My father does the same with my sister. We try to push back with our chopsticks, but my parents' aged Korean hands have an unmatched dexterity. We take five bites for every one of theirs. They watch us eat, then pile on more. When they see that we're stuffed, they beam. And though they barely ate, they suddenly look full too.   —Royce Park

I Got My Father-in-Law
in the Divorce

I met my new boyfriend's father at their family holiday party; we sat in a corner, gabbing intensely. Hugging him goodbye, I thought, "I'm going to marry your son." I did. When my father-in-law retired, we met occasionally for breakfast; now it's monthly. I told him when I was conflicted about my marriage. He held my hand. When my ex and I separated two years ago, he said, "Don't worry; I would never come between you and my dad." "You misunderstand," I said. "You can't. I get Norman in the divorce. You get visitation."

—Alia Covel

What to Do with
the Last Three Hours

We thought we'd heard a flicker of a heartbeat, but it was gone now. Our doctor stared at the screen for an eternity before advising us to evacuate the now nonviable pregnancy. We were to come back in three hours. What to do with the last three hours of my pregnancy? My husband took me to the nearby driving range. With each swing, we hit out our frustration and pain. At 2 p.m., my husband held my hand and stroked my hair as our baby left my body. I had never felt more loved by him than in that moment.   —Amanda Lockwood

The Treasures
He Will Leave Behind

For one week in 40 of his springs, my father searched the shore for shells. My sister tried to keep up; my brother drew in the sand with sticks. I followed behind, collecting the broken shells my father tossed aside. Now we guide our father's hands over his old treasures. I read him the shells' names: pear whelk, leafy jewel box, ponderous ark. Suffering from Parkinson's and dementia, my father simply listens, closes his eyes and smiles. Soon, my siblings and I will search the shore once more, desperate to find what the sea and my father have left behind.

—Carrie Friedman

We Won't Finish
This Story Together

The nineteen-year age difference appalled my
mother: "It will kill your father!" Yet my father
approved. "We don't always understand what
Gayle does," he said, smiling, at my wedding. "But
it always works out." In time, nobody noticed the
age gap—we certainly didn't. But thirty-four years
on, it's gaping again. We know we won't finish this
story together. I creak a little; he creaks more. Yet
we're still riding the same wave of passion that we
always have: argument, travel, art, a shared table.
We refuse to end with a whimper; we will crash
with happiness.

—Gayle Austen

Dressed up as Pugsley and Wednesday Addams.

New Announcement, New Name, Still Ours

When you were born, we sent announcements—name, weight and date engraved on thick white cards with pale pink stripes and polka dots. "It's a girl," we said. We were thrilled. Now, sixteen years later, so much is new. The pink was wrong. The name was too. This time, we know. It's a boy. There will be no pastel stationery. We are telling everyone face-to-face. He's ours.

—Maria Blackburn

When Cupid Is a Landlord

We met while competing for an apartment. I was trying to get into his head to discourage him from applying for the space, but he thought I was flirting. Fifteen minutes later, when I turned in my application, the landlord thought we were looking for an apartment together. "No, we just met!" I said. "I don't know this guy." "That's too bad," she replied. "You'd make a great couple." I got the apartment; he got my number. Turns out she was right—we've been together for eight years, married for four, and now we hope to adopt a baby.　—Leah Wade

A Shaft of Light

We were 7-year-olds without siblings, living in adjacent Montreal apartments that shared a bathroom light shaft. Margaret had curly, ruddy-brown hair and glasses, and we simply liked each other. As soon as our parentally approved time together ended, we would run to our respective bathrooms, stand on our respective toilet seats and chatter through the windows until called away. Eventually, her family moved out and mine left Canada. Sixty-two years later, I see: That light shaft was our social medium, those windows our screens, in our analog love story.

—Dov Midalia

A Long To-Do List

The night you were discharged from the clinic where we had been both patient and prisoner, you tried to throw yourself into blinding headlights. Days later, I visited you in a new white room. You showed me a list of things you wanted to do. It was long, and I was relieved. You had written "Kiss Greta," and I looked at you, surprised. That's when you checked off the first thing on that list, and I thought of time, how ours had intersected to produce an unpredictable bond and a happiness that we had missed for so long.

—Greta Kerr

Relationships Are Like Shoes

My mother told me that relationships are like shoes: "No matter how beautiful they are or how much you love them, if they don't fit, there will be pain with every step. Nobody will know it but you." There was pain in my relationship with my boyfriend of eight years, but I had ignored it. I finally understood the true meaning of my mother's saying when he cheated on me. I don't hate him or the other woman anymore. I took off the shoes and am free.   —Karleen Chiu

A Cozy, Crowded Bed

My friend June said, "Get rid of the gray. Everyone lies about their age." I kept the gray but pretended I was 71, my younger sister's age. My other friend, Alice, said, "Don't waste your time with these dating sites." Online, not much activity. I wrote to some men; some men wrote to me. Then a man, a professor my age, married forty-four years until his wife died, asked me out. I, also a professor, widowed after thirty-six years, said OK to coffee. Turns out he lives two blocks away. Now the bed is crowded: his wife, my husband, us. It's kind of cozy.

—Nan Bauer-Maglin

Best Investment Ever

I once purchased a penny with a heart cut into it at a New Jersey rest stop. Before going on summer break after my sophomore year of college, I gave it to this guy I was hanging out with and made a joke about not spending it all in one place. Twenty years later, using my husband's car while he's in Florida for our son's baseball tournament, I discover that penny on his key ring. A pretty good return on a one-cent investment. —Melanie McGrath

Watching Other People
Fall for My Boy

I fell in love with a boy when I was only 18. Both of us were raised in conservative Christian households, and we said "I do" at 20. Twelve years and two children later, we're still in love. But I kept falling in love with other people, too. So now we're polyamorous. I have a boyfriend. My husband has a girlfriend. And he and I share a relationship with another woman. What I think I like most is watching other people fall in love with the same boy I fell for years ago. It's like, "Yeah, you get it, right?"

—Jennifer Martin

After Forty-Eight Hours,
It's Time to Move On

Tom, my husband of thirty-one years, died early one January morning from injuries sustained in a fall at home. Two days later, I received an email from a dating service for those over 50. The subject line asked, "Are you ready to try love again?" I burst out laughing. It had to be a coincidence. Or are all the computers trading information? Maybe the consensus on the internet is that after forty-eight hours, it's time to move on. When I stopped laughing, I thought, "I've got to tell Tom. He'll think it's hilarious." Oh. I do that a lot these days.

—Nora Raum

My King in the Uniroyal Jacket

Dad, do you remember when you came home late from work (as you did in those days) and scooped me up out of bed, wrapped me in my blanket and set me on the back of your borrowed motorcycle? We rode to the A&W and sat on a bench under the egg-yolk-yellow lights with root beer floats: the orange awning flapping; the moonlit sky; a childhood that would last a lifetime; the smell of work in your shirt; me, the prince of your moment; and you, the king in your Uniroyal jacket.

—Theodore Groves

We Couldn't Marry,
So She Married a Guy

As we sat close together at a café, I asked her if she was sure. We had been lovers for five years and friends for ten. "My wedding is in two days," she replied. "I hope you can make it." Then she said, "Had you been a guy, we would have two kids by now. Also, married." I smiled, and she smiled back, her expression spelling regret. We were two Filipino women without the right to wed.   —April Casquejo

Burnt Honey

We graduated from the same culinary school but met working together at food events. I developed new food products that she styled for photo shoots. For more than ten years, I ignored my feelings for this beautiful woman: so smart, funny, talented and—married. One night at a cookbook launch party, we stood in a dark studio in Austin, Texas. She told me about her favorite new dish, wings coated with burnt honey. When she touched my arm, my vision tunneled. Nothing I could do. Remembering that moment a month later, I recreated the dish. It was delicious.

—John Bartel

Something to Give

The last time I saw my grandma, she had no idea who I was. She'd lost everything: her memories, her laugh, her weight. She'd shiver constantly. "Cold," she'd whisper. "Cold." I kept trying to give her a blanket, but she'd panic every time and hand it back to me. We repeated this until, finally, she used all her energy to reach out and wrap the blanket around me. For the first time, she relaxed, smiled—perfectly content as she shivered. Even with everything taken from her, she found something to give.

—Julia Camp

He Caught My Sneeze

Early on, during our morning train commute, I was clutching the pole with one hand and my coffee with the other when I felt a sneeze coming on. "I'm going to sneeze!" I said, concerned for my caffeine. Seeing my distress, he whipped his hand under my nose to catch the explosion. We were both disgusted. "I just needed you to take my coffee," I said. "Oh," he said. "I wish I'd thought of that." No longer the early days, now there's a baby on the way. I'm happy I found someone who is willing to get his hands dirty.

—Yasmin Sabir

No More We. Just I.

He asked me to marry him on our first date. Over the next twenty-five years, we (mostly I) raised four daughters while moving between two continents, three countries and seven states. We (mostly he) achieved career success, rising through the corporate ranks. We (mostly I) mourned then transitioned to life with a handicapped child. And then we (both) fell apart, just when we should have been enjoying the fruits of our labor. He left me on April Fools' Day last year, six days after we opened our (now my) dream restaurant. There is no more we. Just I.

—Jennifer Brulé

Saving My Life, and Savoring It

I nervously decided to study abroad the summer before my senior year of college, four years after my struggle with anorexia. My body had healed, but my mind was still at war. Italy charmed me like a lover I hadn't expected to meet. Rome courted me on cobblestone streets. Capri caressed me with its sea. Florence spoon-fed me gelato. In a country far away, my body finally began to feel like home. I had saved my life, but Italy taught me how to savor it.

—Stephanie Kennedy

Glad I Wore My Pink Tennis Shoes

When we met in music theory class, he said he liked my pink tennis shoes. "Thanks," I said. "I wear them so people think I'm athletic!" Shortly after, his roommate died in an accident on the Oregon coast. The year before, I had lost my boyfriend in a car crash. I knew what to do. I brought chili and cornbread. I listened. We became friends, roommates, best friends and then, for me, more. "I'm going to cut to the chase," I said. "We can't live together anymore. I have a huge crush on you." He smiled. It's been two and a half years of joy.

—Chloe Smithson

"Tell Me, Honey"

I have worshiped my older brother my entire life. We are in our 50s now. Last summer he fell ill, gripped by mania, his extraordinary mind betraying him, fueling a paranoia that his wife and I were plotting against him. I wept constantly, wracked with worry. I was desperate to talk about it—once a day, or twenty-seven times—for months. Before my brother's recovery, whenever I would begin a sentence "My brother . . . ," my husband of two decades would put down his phone, coffee, newspaper or briefcase, look into my eyes and say, "Tell me, honey."

—Sarah Brazaitis

Hello, Ruby

Unspeakable pain in my right shoulder sent me to the doctor at 37 weeks pregnant. "HELLP syndrome," she said. Life-threatening. Emergency C-section. Blood transfusions. Liver blood clot. Rare. I wasn't ready to meet my baby girl. I searched for clues in the nurse's eyes, asking her, "Am I going to die? Will I be able to be her mother?" My baby lived. I almost didn't. Weeks followed where I couldn't hold Ruby. I was too weak. Wasn't ready. Didn't want to. Then one day, that tiny girl gave me a half smile. I knew we were going to be OK.

—Stefanie Torres

No Joke

We are both named Phoebe. This means our path to love has been littered with disbelief, laughter and confusion. It was hard enough coming out in a lesbian relationship in our late 20s, but a relationship between two people with the same name? People say, "You're joking, right?" But it's no joke that when we moved the fridge during our kitchen renovation, she saw my rainbow writing on the wall, asking her to marry me. And it's no joke that she said yes. And I'm not joking when I say that my life is very nearly perfect now. —Phoebe Wallner

Breaking Up in a Small Town

Breaking up in a small mountain town is hard. I still crane my neck after every white truck, searching the bed for your scratched black toolbox and the ghosts of us intertwined there, sleeping under younger stars. One day we may have children, but not together. And those children—mine, yours, but not ours—may grow up in the valley where we fell in love. They may even ski after school together. I'll smile at your new truck across the ski hill parking lot. Your long auburn hair will be shorter and grayer, but you'll still wear a mustache, and you'll smile back.

—Michelle DeLong

In front of our gallery; Steve is on the left.

The Forty-Eighth Date

As a lonely gay man who seldom went to bars, gyms or theaters, I resorted to a gay matchmaker. I ate forty-seven meals with forty-seven men, none of them a match. Then I had a dinner with Steve, a man with whom I shared low compatibility on paper but high compatibility in person. During our thirty years together, we formalized our relationship with a Vermont civil union, a New Jersey domestic partnership, a Canadian same-sex marriage and, finally, legal marriage in the United States. We framed each certificate, creating a personal exhibit in the larger gallery of LGBTQ civil rights progress.   —Lou Storey

"Hey" Is Not "Heyy"

"Heyy," his message read. My heart fluttered. One "y" might have left me upset, but the second "y"—that was promising. Such a simple yet ambiguous greeting. Did he want to hang out? Was he going to confess his love? Oh! He was typing. A double text! It was my lucky day. I broke a sweat waiting for his next message. How should I respond? "Hi!"? "I am in love with you"? My message had to show the same amount of interest as his. His second text arrived. "Sorry, didn't mean the extra 'y.'" Oh.

—Julia DiGeronimo

India Is an Ache

Landing in Mumbai feels like releasing a breath I didn't know I had been holding. My husband remembers India as dirt, poverty, noise. I remember the aroma of masala-fried pomfret, the generosity of gruff cabbies saying, "No, madam, you keep the change," daylong cries of crows, hawkers, doorbells. In America, I play music to fill silences. For me, India is no longer a country; it's an ache. I left the place I love for the man I love. It's not a complaint. I'm only saying that sometimes, the most unconditional of loves are also the most inconvenient.

—Kanika Punwani Sharma

She Waters Me Every Day

My girlfriend, Emma, makes me drink water. I don't like it, that magical liquid scientists claim is necessary for survival. If it were up to me, I would start the day with three cups of coffee, then maybe have a mug of tea in the afternoon, followed by a few sips of lemonade with dinner. Alas, it's not my decision. At 4 p.m., Emma asks, "How much water have you had today?" When I feel dizzy, she puts her water bottle in my hands. She loves me, so she waters me like she waters her favorite plant.

—Mary Drue Hall

Noise, Then Silence

My husband and I watched from the driveway as our son and his family of five packed their van for the seven-hour drive home. For a week, our house had thrilled to the sounds of small feet on stairs, stories being read, spoons clinking against cereal bowls. Then my littlest grandchild's tricycle was put into the van's hatch, the door slammed, the engine started. We leaned in for last hugs. As their car backed away, the sense of loss was sudden and sharp. For days, we had been absorbed into the life of this precious family. And now, not.

—Penelope Lemov

The Power of Bitmoji

Once upon a time, my partner sent me a sweet text while I was home caring for our baby. Seeing his Bitmoji avatar elicited an oxytocin surge so strong that my milk let down. If that's not an expression of love, I don't know what is. —Jenn Clifford

The Youngest Legal Scholar

Without family near or money to spare, I brought my newborn with me to law school, placing her on my lap during class. Jane's presence may have distracted other students, but it also brought them joy. (Without a dose of humanity, civil procedure can be rather dry.) Jane never cried—neither in class nor as I wrote papers late into the night, waiting for my medical resident husband to come home. Now my daughter thinks my lawyer job is boring, but her quiet patience made it all possible.

—Kate Vaughan

Letting Go of Signs

Our marriage days old, signs portended disaster. My ring didn't fit. When the jeweler stretched it, it shattered. On our honeymoon, a hurricane struck Cancún. Diverted to Nassau, we fled our hotel because of a fire; the concierge booked us a new room with ceiling plaster littering the bed. While snorkeling, Jim lost his wedding band. He quit searching at dusk. I continued, for years, along other shores. Last summer, I stopped wearing my ring out of laziness. In Scotland for our October anniversary, Jim noticed and felt hurt. But I have let go of signs, symbols. Thirty years is proof enough.

—Linda Lowen

Surviving, Then Thriving

I just had to make sure my daughter, Elizabeth, and I survived. We lived with my mother and grandmother until they died within a year of each other. I was lost and alone with this child, the love of my life. I turned to Mr. Wonderful, who I thought would bring joy back to me. Instead, he brought bruises, broken bones, a more-broken heart. Again I was on my own, failing Elizabeth miserably. For five years, I wandered. Then one day, I cleaned out Elizabeth's backpack and found her essay "Why My Mom Is My Hero." We had survived, and then some.

—Julie McMurray

A Question in the Ashes

Our little river cabin caught on fire from grease burning on the stove. Miles away from the nearest Alabama volunteer fire department, we tried to put out the flames with the garden hose. Hours later, amid the blackened walls and stench of burned furniture and plastic, we finally slept. The next morning, I wept as we stood in what was left of the kitchen. My darling reached up to the sooty ceiling with one finger and wrote, "Will you marry me?" I stopped crying just long enough to reach up and write, "OK."   —Gita Maritzer Smith

Call Your Grandmother

She doesn't realize how one phone call can affect a grandmother who lives far away. It was unexpected but so welcome. My 14-year-old granddaughter called me of her own volition with her just-purchased first phone. It wasn't a text, or a message on Facebook, Twitter, Skype or Instagram, none of which I truly understand. It was a real old-fashioned phone call, her first to me ever. She called to mourn the damage to Notre-Dame because we had been there, just the two of us, on a recent trip to Paris. We shared our sadness and our love.

—Iris Shur

My Son, the Homeowner

My son just bought a house. My 32-year-old with a modest salary saved enough for a down payment. My child who struggled for so long found a first-time-home-buyer assistance program and earned a matching grant. My firstborn whose future I questioned—would he ever become independent?—met with loan officers, talked with bankers, engaged a realtor. My Matthew closed the deal on a two-bed, one-bath bungalow with hardwood floors, a funky kitchen and a screened-in porch. My son, diagnosed with a brain tumor at age 11, exceeds my every expectation.

—Karen DeBonis

To Live and Die in the Dark

In high school, we watched *Brokeback Mountain* in the movie theater, a secret date. The story on the screen was set in rural Wyoming in the early 1960s. We lived in a liberal state, New York, in the mid-2000s. As the movie played, we settled into the theater's darkness, held hands, touched legs. My head rested on his shoulder. When the movie ended and the lights came up, we had already pulled apart. A world away and generations later than the cowboys on the screen, what we shared was also doomed to live and die in the dark. —Seamus Kirst

Together at St. Pancras station in London, after my son's college graduation.

"I Can't Do This on My Own"

As I pushed my shopping cart through the pink gate of our row house in Melbourne and up the street toward the supermarket, my 3-year-old son decided to assert his independence, refusing to step beyond our fence. Knee-deep in single parenthood and at the end of my ability to cajole, coax, encourage or demand, I turned to look him square in the eye. "I can't do this on my own," I said. "We need to work together." He met my gaze, abandoned his tantrum and ran toward me. We have been a team ever since.

—Elizabeth Keen

Sleeping Through the Seasons

In the fall, her feet get cold when we lie in bed, so she curls her legs into me, molding her toes to the insides of my calves. In the winter, she wears fluffy socks and holds my ears because I'm suddenly the cold one. In the spring, as it gets warmer, I reach down into the covers to wrestle off her monstrous socks. My favorite is summer. In the summer, we sleep naked.

—Megan Schippmann

An Open Door

We followed other prospective service-dog teams in a circle. Each time we stopped, Aslan pressed his golden head against my hip. "Choose *me*," his brown eyes seemed to say. "I belong with you." I agreed. But we still had to prove that we could work together as a team. I rolled up to a closed door, Aslan at my side. He tossed that great head of his, pushed the handicapped plate with his nose, then glanced back to make sure I had noticed. That's when I knew he was mine. The door swung open.

—Jeanne Marie McArdle

As Our World Shrinks, Hers Expands

Our 3-month-old decided that she no longer wants to sleep. Not forever, we hope. But for now. As new parents, we are learning, like everyone during this pandemic, to take it one day at a time. While our worlds condense into two-hour sleep stretches and 2,000 square feet of self-isolation, our daughter's world continues to expand. We find solace in her small wonders: her fingers tracing the lines of our faces, her delight in the guitar, our silly dancing, the range of her newfound voice. Today, there is hope in her tiny universe. We hold it fiercely.

—Charity Yoro

Yes, Rabbis Play Pool

My friend wanted to set us up. I said the seventeen-year age gap was too great, and besides, I would never date a rabbi. She brought him to our weekly pub trivia game, "just as a friend, no pressure." Up close, I noticed eye crinkles from a lifetime of smiling, his booming laugh. Later, I saw him walking home in the rain. He accepted my ride offer. Our first date was shooting pool. My non-Jewish friends were incredulous: "Rabbis do that?" Yes, they do. Rabbis shoot pool in dive bars, caulk your tub, hold your gaze and win your heart.

—Tova Tenenbaum

The Dress I Can't Throw Away

When I was 15, I bought a white dress at a store called Tree of Life. I told my best friend that one day, I would marry her in it. We laughed, which hurt me, though I couldn't figure out why. Eventually, I worked it out and told her the truth: None of it had ever been a joke. In the same sentence, she told me that she loved me but we could never happen—girls didn't marry other girls. In 2017, when marriage equality passed in Australia, she was the first person I thought of, my first great love. I've kept the white dress. I don't think I could ever throw it away.

—Eleanor Gerrard

One Small Step for Man, One Giant Leap for Us

If not for the moon landing, romance might have passed us by. It's possible that I, the Scottish cook in the tenement kitchen in Glasgow, would have never met Peter, the American divinity student volunteering there that summer. Serving soup on July 20, 1969, the day Neil Armstrong walked on the moon, I declared the mission a waste of resources. Peter countered that it was a momentous achievement. Arguing passionately, we found attraction amid disagreement. Fifty years on, we still disagree about space exploration, but we celebrate that auspicious day when the moon brought us into the same orbit. 　　　　—Jenny Fleming-Ives

Maybe It Just Stopped Being Good

Maybe he didn't love me from the beginning. Maybe I shouldn't have accepted his mother's engagement ring. Maybe he didn't mean it when he held me close. Maybe I expected too much of him. Maybe we shouldn't have bought that house, built the barn, so carefully tended the chickens and sheep, the roses and raspberries. Maybe we shouldn't have moved to India. Maybe if I hadn't needed him to help me take care of my mother. Maybe if he had been different. Maybe if I had been. Maybe not. But maybe.

—Judith Edmister

He Won't Stop Getting Down on One Knee

We've been married for five years and have two children. We rarely argue, but if we get into an argument in public—walking down the street or in a restaurant—Paul will drop to one knee, take my hand in his, look up at me lovingly and ask, "Will you please forgive me?" Cars begin honking, people stare and the waitress starts ordering a dessert on the house, to my absolute horror. Reminded why I said yes to him in the first place, I say yes again.

—Lauren Gray

Got hitched in Idaho.

Second Time at the Hitching Post

Almost fifty years ago, Sue and I hurriedly married to avoid the embarrassment of being unwed parents in seven months. The ceremony remains a blur, but the declaration of "Until death do us part" was unforgettable. Five years and two children later, we divorced. A few months ago, I was given the prognosis of one to two years of life. When I shared the news with Sue, she offered to care for me. Last month, we remarried. Our daughter was our witness as we declared once again: "Until death do us part."   —Rodney Santos

The Flamingo Connection

Peyton posted a picture with his flamingo, Lisa, wearing a Santa hat. Lisa had an Instagram account, so I followed it. He texted: "I see you following my lawn flamingo on Instagram." I replied: "You tagged it in a photo. What other option did I have?" The texts got longer. Christmas slid to New Year's and eventually to an evening watching the stars. I asked him why he'd texted me; he asked why I'd responded. We both knew. I'm thankful for that flamingo. "She's the only girl I'll ever love," he once said. But that's not true anymore.

—Kate Bellows

Any Color, Any Day

"You can have three colors if you want," I said to my 3-year-old daughter as patrons and aestheticians looked on, horrified. Was I truly allowing my toddler to get a multicolored pedicure? What kind of a self-absorbed monster was I raising? Just two years earlier, my child had been fighting for her life, spending months in the hospital, undergoing multiple procedures. Her feet and hands swallowed up by giant IVs, she nursed unimaginable pain for a tiny person. Today she is thriving. She can paint her nails any color, any day, for the rest of her life.

—Gabriela Revilla Lugo

Our Four Secret Years

I didn't want to fall in love with her. I had a husband. I led worship at my church. Naturally, my affection was unnatural. Then why did it feel right? How could love be wrong? Perhaps only those who have tried not to fall in love understand fully why it's called falling. You can't stop it. Can't feel the earth beneath your feet. Leaving our husbands, we had four secret years. Then she left me for a man. She couldn't be open about us. Not "strong enough," she said. Fifteen years later, I still cry.

—Paula Wescott

Twenty-Two Minutes Without Oxygen

After seven days in a coma following twenty-two minutes without oxygen during an unfortunately named instance of "cardiac death," my husband began to flutter his eyelids. My father and I had been waiting, hopeful but frightened. We wondered: Will he be able to talk? To walk? To feed or bathe himself? The predictive tests hadn't been encouraging. So we stared, and after a while my husband's blue eyes focused on mine. Then he sputtered and coughed. We stared. He blinked. We stared. Finally, I whispered, "How are you, love?" He sighed and said, "Well, I've been mostly dead all day."

—Lisa Petty

Three Ceremonies,
Two Daughters, No Religion

We met during our first year of college. By our final year, we were inseparable but kept our relationship secret. Our families couldn't know. Kruttik was Hindu; I was Muslim. An impossible union. When my mother eventually found out, my family acted like a loved one had died. Seven years of tears, family estrangement and emotional torture later, Kruttik and I married in three ceremonies in three Indian cities, trying to keep the Hindu and the Muslim gods happy. That was twelve years ago. We have two daughters and a new sense of family now. We are also atheists.

—Zainab Zaki

What My Twin Understands

My twin brother has autism and can't talk much. I'm a writer. Mother says I sucked out all the words from him in the womb. When we were 12, I walked into my brother's room and simply said, "I'm gay." I had never said those words out loud before. I figured he couldn't tell anyone even if he wanted to. He looked at me, his expression unchanged. I started to cry. My twin didn't understand what I had told him, or what being gay meant, but he saw that I was sad and reached out for my hand.

—Sarah Emily Baum

"I Miss Daddy"

My 5-year-old came back from the weekend at his father's house wearing his father's hat. He wouldn't take it off. "I miss Daddy," he said. There were no tears. No tantrums. No whining. He stated the facts. It just was, and he accepted it. I wondered at my son's strength, at his heartache. My parents aren't divorced. I don't know what it's like. That night he fell asleep sucking his thumb and wearing his father's hat.

—Amy Okura

Vision Optional

Fifteen years ago, meeting online meant sharing stories about yourself rather than swiping right. John and I hit it off instantly, jokes and anecdotes flowing. After three weeks of messaging, I was more than interested. He was hilarious, intelligent, successful and kind. And, it turns out, visually impaired—so visually impaired that future blindness is a possibility. I closed my laptop to consider, giving myself twenty-four hours to think, but I needed only two. Blindness wasn't a choice for him; why should it be for me? Hearts required, vision optional.

—Jennifer Haendel

A Rescue Cat Rescued Me

I met my cat, Talula, on a cold night in 2004 when I was too broke to take Amtrak and too sick to eat dinner. She had been hit by a car but saved by a friend. I was dying from anorexia. I took New Jersey Transit to Philadelphia to pick her up, and I kept her warm with a sweater and sang to her the whole ride home. In New York, she slept on my head, sat on my lap and helped me recover. It took fourteen years.

—Rena Silverman

He Uses My Head as an Armrest

He's 6 foot 5—taller than Steph Curry. I'm as tall as five Subway sandwiches. Although I prefer the guys I date to be taller than me, this wasn't what I had in mind. There are challenges. Reaching for his hand reminds me of my kindergarten days, my arm extended at full length to tug at my mother's skirt. When waiting in line, he sometimes uses my head as an armrest. Yes, he's the type of person I would hate to sit behind at concerts or movies, but, luckily, he chooses to be by my side.

—Roan Raymundo

Nothing Lacking

The day my first child, Aviva, was born, my mother had a double mastectomy. A day after I brought Aviva home, my mother was released from the hospital. She came straight to my house. When she walked in, I was breastfeeding. My breasts, white and plump and full of milk, were exposed in an almost teasing display of what my mother lacked. I cried tears of sadness. Seeing her newborn grandchild, my mother cried tears of joy. —Liat Katz

Please, Tell Me About My Brother

I look at his girlfriend with envy. She knows him like I wish I did. Tell me about him, I want to say. Tell me how he likes his coffee, when he last cried, how he looks when sleeping. Tell me how he says good night, if he writes poems, how he is with your family. Tell me what he's said about his childhood, his parents, his sister. Tell me if he wants children, a dog, a house in Japan. Tell me his theories about life, his nightmares, his secrets. Please, I want to say. Tell me about my brother.   —Lucy Mae Coulson

Here's a Chair for You

I was excited for my eldest son's engagement party. I was also nervous, having not seen my ex-husband in five years. Mid-celebration, I looked up from my cup of cold coconut soup to see my 8-year-old son from my second marriage, Asher, carry a chair over to my ex. Crouching on the grass beside his second wife's seat, my ex startled at the sudden chair behind him. Then he turned to Asher—a child who wouldn't exist had I not broken my ex-husband's heart—and smiled.

—Gayle Brandeis

The Itch Persists

Tired, we decided to lie down in Chicago's gorgeous Graceland Cemetery. I rested my head on his chest, relaxing into his breath. I tried my best to ignore the itchiness of the grass, the itch to explore the what-ifs of someone else. This is it now. How long will it last? Till death? —Hannah Davis Atkinson

My Mother's Hands in Mine

I took my mother's hands as she lay dying at age 91. I beheld her fingers. Long and graceful. Manicured and polished coral, even on the last day of her life. Her hands were not always so pretty when she had worked typewriters, the earth in her many gardens, and snarls out of her children's hair. These were hands that had washed, folded, mended, ironed, stacked, and stowed ceaselessly. Now they lay warm and still as life left her. Gradually, she uncoupled her hands from mine and was gone.

—Shelley Meader Walinski

Our Ages Added Up Perfectly

In 1990, I joined Herb's campaign for South Carolina governor. Herb wanted to overturn the provision in the state constitution that prohibited atheists from holding public office. We met in person, then fell in love via phone and letters during the summer. I worried about telling him my age. When he asked, I said, "Fifty-two. And you?" "Forty-eight." We lost the election but helped to overturn the law. After we wed, I asked, "What did you think when I told you my age?" He said, "I thought 52 and 48 make 100." Did I mention he was a mathematics professor?

—Sharon Fratepietro

The day we got engaged. I'm on the right. Hazel is on the left.

I See It, Too

The camera can add 10 pounds. It can also take off 10 if you angle it right. "Honestly? I wish you were a little thinner," one Craigslist date said. "You're attractive, but I'm not attracted to you," said another. I felt like giving up. I could resign myself to the company of dogs, getting a new one every thirteen years or so until I . . . Unwilling to finish that thought, I looked directly into the lens and ventured online one last time. She saw beauty. I see it too.   —Caitlin O'Toole

"A Couple of What?"

"If you cry when I die, I'm going to haunt you," Rick said. "You're going to have to haunt me," I replied. Months later, as I walked around the apartment we were supposed to share, I shouted, "Where are you, you bastard?" When Rick took his last breath, my heart crumpled. No romance between us. We barely hugged. "You're a lovely couple," people would say. "A couple of what?" we'd respond. We were best friends, often found sitting on the couch, laughing like idiots. "Rick, we're stupid," I'd say. He'd answer, "Yes, but we're happy."

—Betty Adorno

Hugs Can Skip a Generation

My Korean parents didn't grow up with physical affection from their parents, so they didn't know how to give it. Instead, they patted us on the back—the more vigorous the pat, the more they meant they loved us, were proud of us. I now watch my children, raised with uninhibited physical demonstrations of love, hug and kiss my parents, unabashedly telling them "I love you." My parents physically reciprocate with their grandchildren in a way they still can't with their own children. But that's OK. We had the shoulder pats.

—Haley M. Hwang

Our Return to Tenderness

I used to lift you overhead, laughter reverberating from your infant throat. "You're going to be a party girl," I cooed. Your childhood was no party, though. Custody battles. Your other mother won. At age 10, you were returned to me. During your teen years, that party girl let loose. Defiance, slammed doors, a DUI. Finally, you asked for help. "My baby's inside there," I said, pointing to your heart. "Take care of her." Five months sober now, you say, "Show me how." Once, you had no patience for tender words. Today you drink them in.

—Tzivia Gover

Seeing Her in Me

"I'm sorry for your loss," people say. As if you're lost, like a forgotten wallet or misplaced keys. A phrase used to empathize, to quell unease. I have said it too—about pets and strangers, but never about you. I find you in my deep-set eyes and the cheekbones below. My hands match yours thirty years ago. I see you in my summer tan that's dark by mid-July, and in the lines that arc around my mouth if I laugh or cry. No, I haven't lost you, Mom. That could never be. You're present everywhere, most of all in me.   —Alicia Gabe

I Married a "Yes" Man

The sniffer dog at Sydney Airport detected the forgotten apple buried deep in my husband's backpack. (Two trips before, my dearest had mistakenly ticked all the "yes" boxes on the immigration card. Tuberculosis: yes. Biological specimens: yes. Firearms: yes. Illicit drugs: yes. "Mate," sighed the immigration officer. "The fellow before you only spoke German, and he got it right.") I worked my jet-lagged child's foot into a sneaker, wondering how it came to pass that I am saddled with such a travel partner. Oh yes, it was a proposal—at an airport.

—Kate Palmer

We Know Where We Are, and It's Not Paris

At Paddy's Clam House in Manhattan, the maître d' sat us in a cozy, poorly lit corner. Newly engaged, I leaned over and gave Gail a simple peck on the cheek. The maître d' charged forward and said, in a disapproving tone, "Where do you think you are, Paris?" The question became code for furtive kisses in unanticipated places. Thirty-eight years later, we were at an airport in Paris, standing in line for our connecting flight to Kiev. I turned to Gail and, without a word, we smiled, kissed and exclaimed in unison, "Where do you think you are?"

—Jay Chaskes

If You Need Light in Your Life, Call an Electrician

My ex left me with two young children and a house in disrepair. I couldn't face my children's searching eyes and endless questions, but I could call an electrician. John appeared the next day. Sharing a ladder, we struggled to mount a ceiling fan in the waning light of a summer evening. It was then, John said, in seeing my belly peeking from my shirt, that he fell for me, our shadows dancing on the walls. Apparently, the entire house had to be rewired. John made the right connections, and eighteen years later, the light remains. —April Silva

Good Thing He Didn't
Give Up His Seat for Me

It was unsettling to find myself still single at 36. A married couple who had met at my 30th birthday party (lucky them) had a dinner party one night, serving only cheese and wine. I nearly missed a flight the next morning, vomiting from that "dinner." Somehow I made it on the plane. With an eye to the bathroom, I asked the tall man in the aisle seat to trade for the window. "No; the legs . . . ," he said. Resigned, I navigated to my seat. But he felt bad. We talked. Turns out he was 36 and single too. Our daughter is now 13.　　　　　　　—Leecia Manning

My mother, looking regal at my childhood home in Detroit, having just turned 93.

When Shame Leads to Kindness

My mother and I were driving through Detroit when we stopped at a light and noticed a blind man attempting to cross a busy street. My mother told me to go help him, but I—a shy, baffled teenager—refused. She got out and helped the man cross, then we drove on. My shame lingered until decades later in Los Angeles when I noticed a blind man trying to cross Vine Street. I stopped and helped him, shutting down five lanes of traffic. Driving off, I heard people clapping and tooting their horns. Thank you for your example, Mother.

—Thomas Drotar

I Loved Their Son in Secret

The sound of the garage door pulled us apart, a grating alarm signaling that his parents were home early. Wide-eyed and stammering, he gathered my things and heaved them—and me—out the back door. I re-dressed and tiptoed around the house, stopping beneath his parents' window just as their light flicked on, the small shaft of light finding me like a spotlight on an escaped prisoner. If only they had opened the blinds, they would have seen the boy who loved their son in secret—but they never did, and we never met, and the light went off.

—Topher Daniel

Still in My Garden

When we met in December, he told me he couldn't commit. In January, I told him I loved him. In March, he planted a sunflower in my New Orleans garden that dwarfed the other plants, stealing their sun. In July, I tore his eleven-footer down, struggling to sever its massive roots. Victorious, I posed for a picture with his sunflower's head. In September, he pulled up the picture over drinks. "That's your sunflower," I said. "I know," he said. I meant to free myself, my garden, of him, but he's still here on our one-year anniversary of not actually dating.

—Marcelle Beaulieu

Finding a Date in Divorce Group

In Massachusetts, if you're divorcing and have children under 18, you must complete a parenting program. For five Wednesday nights, my friend and I were buzzed into the local middle school, where we sat at small desks among other newly single parents: the crying blonde in scrubs, the angry landscaper, the excited executive. I brought gin in an orange Nalgene bottle. He hadn't eaten for days. On the night I saw my son's geography project propped up on the classroom radiator, we kissed behind the clothing donation bin, and I thought I would die of grief and hope. —Bethany Dorau

Regaining Her Words

My 85-year-old mother was trying to regain her ability to speak after a stroke. I brought family photographs to the hospital. I'd say the names of loved ones, and she would attempt to repeat them. After days of frustration, she began to correctly, proudly and loudly say the names when the photographs were produced. One day, she started humming the tune of an old nursery rhyme, and I joined her in recalling the words. A nurse came to the door and asked what we were doing. My mother smiled and said, "We . . . are doing . . . love."   —Tracy Siani

Here with our daughter, Adelaide, our newborn son, Leo, and our chihuahua, Clarence.

Her Fabulous Hair

We don't remember the name of the East Village bar where we met, but I remember the first thing I ever said to her: "How much money do you spend on that hair?" "Nothing," Melissa said. "I went gray in my early 20s." Now we're five years and two children from that blind date, and strangers think we're grandparents. We fell in love late in life, with decades of experiences under our belts: city living, careers, travel, parties, parents battling cancer. I just got lucky choosing her favorite topic as my opening salvo.   —Michael LeFort

Living in the Light

I was old and transgender but not out. I was searching the world in the dark with a small flashlight, lying in bed alone, smartphone in hand, thinking, "What am I doing?" I downloaded an app and began writing: "Does anyone want to talk to a trans woman?" Before Diane and I met in person, she said, "I thought maybe I'd meet a friend. I didn't think I'd find love." We found love. We dated. We married. I transitioned to live as my true self, and we started a new life in the light.

—Gia Sanchez

Strength Training

My first personal training session was less than twenty-four hours after my boyfriend of four years broke up with me. I couldn't breathe—or cancel. I balked at the weight the trainer asked me to pull, push, carry, grab, move. "You're stronger than you think," he said. I cried. Four weeks later, I cried different tears as he took a video of me getting my chin over the bar for the first time in my weak-armed life. My trainer was barely more than an acquaintance, but he taught me how to pull myself up.

—Marilyn Vaccaro

The Prairie Dog of My Dreams

When I was young, my dreams often featured snippets of prairie dogs; they would appear intermittently, like commercial breaks. It was strange, but that's how my dreams played. In my 20s, I found myself talking until dawn with my roommate, Ken. One night, a silly question came up: "If you could be any animal, what would you be?" "A prairie dog," Ken said. After that conversation, the commercial breaks went dark. Thirty years later, I'm still married to the man (or prairie dog) of my dreams.

—Ava Chinn

Water Rushing Beneath Us

The sign read: CROSS FORD AT YOUR OWN RISK. "What's a ford?" I asked. "A low water bridge," you said, slowing the car. The ford was submerged, but you drove onto it and opened your door. Water rushed beneath the car. "Open yours," you said. I sat, frozen. You laughed. I opened the door an inch, then more. "Now listen." The sound of the creek filled the car. I breathed in wet grass, mud, dead leaves. I reached down and let the water run through my fingertips. Life with you, I knew, would be different.   —Jessica Braun

When a Chandelier
Falls on Your Head

All I ever wanted was a dog, but Carlito was allergic and unmovable. I married him anyway, certain that love would prevail. One night while we were eating with friends in a Manhattan restaurant, a 50-pound chandelier broke out of the ceiling, partly striking my head. I bled; Carlito wept. When the EMT told everyone I would live, Carlito's friend leaned over my stretcher and whispered, "Now's the time to ask for anything . . . " We named the puppy Chandelier. Carlito sneezed every day of our dog's life, but he didn't care one bit.   —Shari Simpson

Two Astronomy Nerds

It was supermoon night, the kind astronomy nerds long for. I had an exam the next day and my nose in a biology textbook when this strawberry blonde girl asked if anyone knew how to get to the observatory. It's a through-the-woods kind of thing, but I did, in fact, know how to get there. We hiked with phone flashlights along two trails to the top of the hill. Looking at our moonlit shadows, we sat silent. Heading back, we got lost, and I traded a leaf for her number.

—Ethan Bradley

Flirting Before Coffee

Every morning on the short walk to my neighborhood café, I would try to think of something clever to say to the cute cashier who worked there. It was the hardest thing I had ever tried to do: flirt before coffee. Usually I mumbled something unintelligible about working late or my car getting towed. One morning, I noticed her name tag and said, "Hi, Anu," mispronouncing her name. Luckily, there was a banana sticker on my shirt. "I'm Chiquita," I said. Twenty-eight years later, I'm still Chiquita. Turns out I didn't have to say something clever. I just had to say something.

—Rob Thoms

It's OK to Feel Fear

My daughter couldn't fall asleep because she was scared. Nothing helped—not the back rub or child valerian drops or my assurance of no monsters. She spiraled into hiccuping sobs. I pleaded, "Honey, everyone's scared of something." "No! You're not scared of anything." "I am!" "What are you scared of?" I tried to think of some comforting half-truth. "See? You're not scared of anything!" "I am," I whispered. "I'm scared of . . . getting old . . . and my anger. And consumerism, stupidity, children without attention spans, distracted drivers and—" "OK. Have good dreams, Mama." She turned and fell asleep.   —Karen Rizzo

A photo from our wedding in Llandovery, Wales. Wendy is on the left.

She Stretched Like My Cat

Wendy was one of my favorite single-mum friends. She had a disconcertingly careless way of stretching that reminded me of my cat. Her stomach was toned, and her T-shirts were tight. One day, she turned up at a friend's house with a girlfriend. I was so cross that I started avoiding her. She assumed I was homophobic. I missed her optimism and her endless enthusiasm for gossip and chocolate. Eventually, I tossed a coin and invited her over for a drink. I was terrified. We got married last year. Turns out, all that stretching hadn't been so careless after all.

—Joanna Lambert

Don't Blame This on Mercury

We were sitting on his memory-foam mattress when he admitted to being a bad boyfriend. "The moon is pulling different elements of my sign," he said. "It's Mercury in retrograde." A feeling of dread crept into my throat and held it closed. I wondered why the moon had never pulled me away from him. I looked up and saw a shiny ripped condom wrapper on his nightstand. It wasn't ours. Was it a sign? I silently got up and left because I had my own two feet, and nothing in the universe could stop me.

—Laurel Kho

Less Lovable Than Lobster

Despite a drawn-out divorce, I frequently have reveries about a certain endearing trait of my former wife's. When half asleep, she would often make funny statements in her altered state. Example No. 1: She: "Turn off the light." Me: "I did." She: "No." She points to the window. Me: "That's the moon." She: "Then turn off the moon." Example No. 2, my favorite: As she snuggled up to me, eyes closed, semiconscious, she murmured, "I love you more than anything." A pause. "Except lobster."

—Gene Keyes

A Lack of Symmetry

We were in my college apartment after several weeks of hooking up when he said, "You feel good. Is this good?" "Yeah," I said. "This is good. I feel good." And he said, "I'm happy." And I said, "I'm happy." And he said, "I like this." And I said, "I like you." That was it—not in a "that was it; they fell in love" kind of way, but in a "that was it; he saw the possibility of connection beyond my bed and got scared and ran away" type of way.　—Sarah Marlin

He Waited Until Morning

It was Christmas Eve in the intensive care unit. My husband was unresponsive. I put my head on his bed and dozed off. When I awoke, it was 2 a.m. Christmas morning. Death was coming, and I was afraid. I caressed his hand and talked to him. "I don't want to drive home alone in the dark and cold. Can you wait until dawn to pass on?" I got in bed with him; our souls met. Peace. The sun came up, and my husband took his last breath. His final gift to me was the gift of light.

—Cathy Lickteig Makofski

Here I am with my youngest, who is now grown up!

Suddenly Happy

My husband, two young daughters and I were a close and happy family. One July 4, my husband suffered heart complications and eventually died. It was a bleak and traumatic time for us. I operated on autopilot, managing my daily tasks robotically. With little hope in her voice, my youngest daughter asked, "Mom, will we ever be happy again?" I looked at her and promised, "We will be happy again." My words were really a prayer. Years passed. One day, my youngest suddenly declared, "Mom, you promised we'd be happy again, and we are."

—Lois Cooper

Linked by a Stranger from Brooklyn

I'm a geneticist. At a conference where I was presenting, I spit into a tube for one of those DNA tests that are now all the craze. How fitting but surprising to discover not one but six half siblings. I grew up with one full sister. Our parents, now deceased, never mentioned a sperm donor. I suppose that's how they quietly managed infertility in the 1950s. Although I was initially incredulous, I delight in the fact that, more than half a century ago, an anonymous man from Brooklyn gave us the gift of life and, years later, each other.

—Ricki Lewis

There's a Logic to Love

As an engineer, I believe that problems have logical solutions. To solve my relationship problem, I needed to structure it. Standing at my boyfriend's whiteboard with a marker and a flowchart I'd drawn, I asked him questions, tracing his answers down the chart. He was happy but wasn't sure he could fall in love with me. The chart said "Break up," so we did. I went back to him, promising to love myself enough for both of us. It didn't work. We broke up again. Love is simple. The flowchart and your heart must lead to the same answer: "Stay."

—Jack Simmons

My Polygamist Ancestor and Me

My middle name is Traugott, after my only polyga-
mist ancestor. At 36, I came out as gay, divorced my
wife and left the Church of Jesus Christ of Latter-
day Saints. At 37, I began dating a man. At 42, we
married. A year later, we've entered the stormy
landscape of polyamory. We have each other, our
children and boyfriends. I never thought I would
have anything more in common with Traugott
than an odd name. Now I wonder: Could he and
his two wives have given me relevant advice, a map
for my new love life? Oh, sweet Jesus, the irony.

—Shawn Bitters

Making Friends When You're Over 40

I never see my old friends anymore. Neither does my wife. The extended punk-rock "family" of our youth is long gone. We've all drifted apart physically and emotionally. Our jobs changed. Our responsibilities changed. We changed. Making friends when you're over 40 is hard. There isn't much to bond over. The new connections we do form are tenuous, easily disrupted by the slightest inconvenience. Are relationships transactional? Do we simply have little left to offer? My wife and I feel alone, but at least we are alone together. We cling to each other more tightly each year, hoping the other is enough.

—Daniel Lee Perea

Bye-Bye, "Family" Minivan

The "family" minivan—that he said we needed but that I should buy, for road trips to visit his son in Los Angeles and his daughter in Santa Barbara, and to take our two boys camping and biking and skiing; the "family" minivan that he encouraged me to purchase just the year before, when he knew what he was doing and with whom, and so knew that we were over, doomed, but was too afraid to say, and for which I later blamed him every time I looked in my driveway—has been sold.

—Kyrie Robinson

What We Do in the End

"Your sister is in the hospital," my mother said over the phone. "You need to come home." I had no idea that Jenny, a 44-year-old suburban mother, would be dead from prescription opioids just six days later. Although blindsided by her fatal addiction, I was grateful for those final days in the hospital: feeding my sister, shuffling her to the bathroom, singing show tunes (her eyes always closed) and telling her I loved her. That's what we do in the end: the messy, tender, heartbreaking things. We are our best selves, even if it's too late.   —Kelly O'Connor

Up in the Air

Both flight attendants, we met while working a flight to Seattle, Laura's home city. She told me I made her sweat, paying attention to her like she was a first-class passenger. I said it was just the polyester uniform. On our layover, we drank wine and ate Thai food. I spent the night at her house instead of in my airport hotel room. Seven years later, we married. Now when we find ourselves on the same flight, we sometimes pretend we are strangers meeting for the first time, just to keep things fresh. She says I still make her sweat. —Dawn Grace

An Opening in the Fence

The day we buried our father, the eccentric neighbor who had terrified us as children appeared at our mother's door. He grunted condolences with a shake of his head: "A good man. A bloody good man." As our mother's billowing grief subsided over the years, we noticed that a section of the fence between her yard and his had disappeared. A path developed. For two decades, that path mapped the unlikeliest of friendships and led to a quiet, unexpected love. Our neighbor won't walk that path again. Our mother grieves for another bloody good man.

—Kate Murphy

Lobster and Loon Song

Each of us had come to the lake with our hearts cracked open and picked clean. I waited tables at the resort where city dwellers came for lobster and loon song. He washed the dishes I passed him across the kitchen's steel table. He reached out to me with his quiet, gloved hands. I offered him shells and husks, my hopeful smile. After work, we met by the water. If we were patient, across the lake's untroubled sheen came the voice of the loon, the peace we had traveled far to find, a flash of fire-flies as his eyes met mine. —Nicola Waldron

Into the Snow for Chocolate

It was a snowy New York City winter. My husband, dog and I were living in a fourth-floor walk-up on East Eighty-Fourth Street. I woke up one night at 2 a.m. with an intense craving for chocolate. I woke my husband, Vic, asking him if we had any, though I knew we didn't. He looked at me, said nothing, got out of bed, put on his snow gear and left. A half hour later he returned, silently handing me a large box filled with M&M's and Chunky bars. Without a word, he went back to sleep. That's love.

—Ruth Ress

My Nearly 90-Year-Old Boyfriend

I didn't think I'd be dating in my 80s. My guy, pushing 90, is even older than me. Saturday nights consist of burgers and beers, *SNL* and a shared bed. When we're not together, we're on the phone, worried when one of us gets sick, more worried than we were when we were young—and immortal. He calls me his girlfriend. I call him my boyfriend. We have no plans to marry, live together, buy a house, have a baby. We don't think about the future except to hope we'll be here tomorrow. It's now that matters. That's all.

—Phyllis Raphael

Acknowledgments

With thanks to Allison McGeehon, Amanda Urban, Anya Strzemien, Bonnie Wertheim, Brian Rea, Caitlin O'Keefe, Caroline Que, Cathi Hanauer, Choire Sicha, Gregory Miller, Jessica White, Jordan Cohen, Lia Ronnen, Nancy Murray, Shoshana Gutmajer, Sibylle Kazeroid, Suet Chong, Tracy Ma and, above all, the writers whose stories are featured in this book.

About the Editors

DANIEL JONES has edited Modern Love in The New York Times since the column began in 2004. He appears weekly on the *Modern Love* podcast and is a consulting producer on Amazon Studios' *Modern Love* streaming series. His nonfiction books include *Modern Love: True Stories of Love, Loss, and Redemption* and *Love Illuminated: Exploring Life's Most Mystifying Subject (with the Help of 50,000 Strangers),* and he is the author of a novel, *After Lucy.* Find him on Twitter at @danjonesnyt.

MIYA LEE began interning for Modern Love in 2014. After graduating magna cum laude from Columbia University and completing an editorial internship at Farrar, Straus and Giroux, Miya joined The New York Times as the Modern Love projects assistant. In this role, she evaluates submissions to Modern Love, selects and edits Tiny Love Stories, and is involved in all aspects of Modern Love's franchise: books, events, podcasting and television. Find her on Twitter at @yayamilee.

Photographs courtesy of:
Page 10: Susan Anderson; page 16: Anjali Walia; page 24: Wesley Rowell; page 34: Joyce
Simon; page 44: Elizabeth Mackey; page 52: Molly Welton; page 60: Kat Lieu; page 68:
Walter Korynkiewicz; page 78: Fantasia Norse and "a nice stranger at Vinatería restaurant
in Harlem, New York City"; page 88: Maria Blackburn; page 110: Wayne Hollendonner;
page 124: David Keen; page 134: Dana Santos; page 152: Hazel Payne; page 162: Thomas
Drotar; page 168: Michelle Lavelle; page 178: Lisa Price; page 184: Burkina Cooper.

Library of Congress Cataloging-in-Publication Data

Names: Jones, Daniel, 1962– editor. | Lee, Miya, editor.
Title: Tiny love stories : true tales of love in 100 words or less / edited by Daniel Jones
and Miya Lee of Modern love in The New York times. Other titles: New York times.
Description: New York : Artisan, a division of Workman Publishing Co., Inc. [2020]
Identifiers: LCCN 2020020283 | ISBN 9781579659912 (hardcover)
Subjects: LCSH: Love—Anecdotes. | Interpersonal relations—Anecdotes.
Classification: LCC BF575.L8 T575 2020 | DDC 813/.0850806—dc23
LC record available at https://lccn.loc.gov/2020020283

Design by Suet Chong

Artisan books are available at special discounts when purchased in bulk for premiums
and sales promotions as well as for fund-raising or educational use. Special editions or
book excerpts also can be created to specification. For details, contact the Special Sales
Director at the address below, or send an e-mail to specialmarkets@workman.com.

For speaking engagements, contact speakersbureau@workman.com.

Published by Artisan
A division of Workman Publishing Co., Inc.
225 Varick Street
New York, NY 10014-4381
artisanbooks.com

Artisan is a registered trademark of Workman Publishing Co., Inc.

Published simultaneously in Canada by Thomas Allen & Son, Limited

Printed in China

First printing, November 2020

1 3 5 7 9 10 8 6 4 2